Marco and Giulio Maestro
Riddle City, USA!
A Book of Geography Riddles

HarperCollins *Publisher*

Library of Congress Cataloging-in-Publication Data
Maestro, Marco.
   Riddle City, USA: A book of geography riddles / Marco and Giulio Maestro.
      p.   cm.
   Summary: A collection of original riddles involving city and state names, important
rivers and parks, and other famous places in the United States.
   ISBN 0-06-023368-0. — ISBN 0-06-023369-9 (lib. bdg.)
   1. Riddles, Juvenile.   2. United States—Geography—Juvenile humor.   [1. Riddles.
2. United States—Geography—Miscellanea.]   I. Maestro, Giulio. II. Title.
PN6371.5.M23   1994   93-16665
818'.5402—dc20   CIP
                                                                                       AC

1 2 3 4 5 6 7 8 9 10
❖
First Edition

Here's How to Use This Book

All the riddles in this book are about places in the United States. If you read the riddles carefully, you'll find clues in the questions, and you can use the map on the next two pages to help you find the answers.

Remember, the answers all have to do with *city names*, *state names*, and *important rivers*, *parks*, and *famous places* in the United States.

The answers are at the bottom of each page, along with some interesting facts about the places in the riddles.

Every state is mentioned at least once in this book. See if you can find yours. You'll have fun learning about United States geography, and then you can use these riddles to stump your friends!

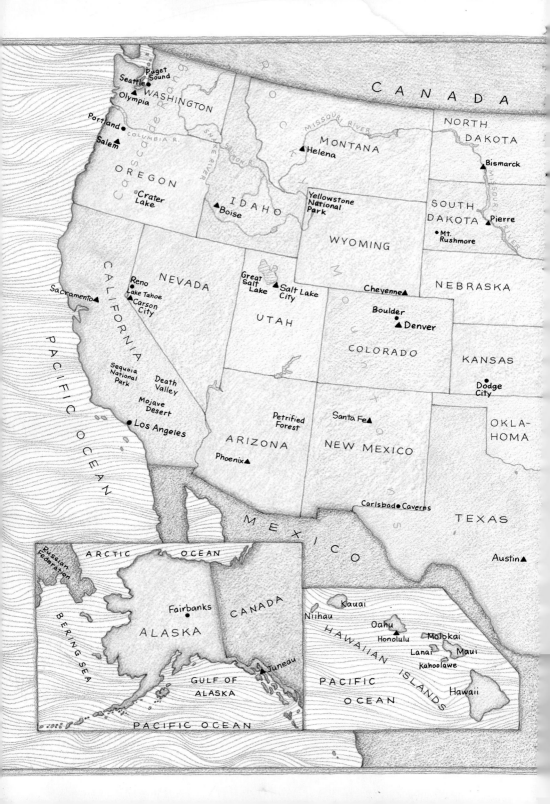

CANADA

PUGET SOUND
Seattle
WASHINGTON
Olympia
Portland
Salem
OREGON
Crater Lake
COLUMBIA R.
SNAKE RIVER
IDAHO
Boise

MONTANA
Helena
MISSOURI RIVER
Yellowstone National Park
WYOMING

NORTH DAKOTA
Bismarck
SOUTH DAKOTA
Pierre
Mt. Rushmore

Reno
Lake Tahoe
Carson City
NEVADA
Sacramento
CALIFORNIA

Great Salt Lake
Salt Lake City
UTAH

Cheyenne
Boulder
Denver
COLORADO

NEBRASKA

KANSAS
Dodge City

Sequoia National Park
Death Valley
Mojave Desert
Los Angeles
ARIZONA
Phoenix
Petrified Forest
Santa Fe
NEW MEXICO

OKLAHOMA

Carlsbad Caverns
TEXAS

MEXICO

Austin

PACIFIC OCEAN

ARCTIC OCEAN
Russian Federation
BERING SEA
Fairbanks
ALASKA
CANADA
Juneau
GULF OF ALASKA
PACIFIC OCEAN

Kauai
Niihau
Oahu
Honolulu
Molokai
Lanai
Maui
Kahoolawe
HAWAIIAN ISLANDS
PACIFIC OCEAN
Hawaii

The U.S.A.

▲ State Capitals

What city hatched in Illinois?

Chick-ago. A fact that pops out about Chicago is that it's the third-largest city in the whole United States! (New York, New York, is number one, and Los Angeles, California, is number two.)

What state is almost always hot and dry?

Arid-zona. You'll almost never catch a chill in Arizona, which often has temperatures over 100° Fahrenheit. Arizona is also one of the driest states; only Nevada gets less rain each year.

What Florida city sounds just like soda pop?

Pensa-cola! Pensacola is in the northwestern part of Florida, a state with a subtropical climate. That means that it's a good idea to have some cold soda on hand to drink!

Why was the New York tabby so talented?

She was from the Cat-skill Mountains! Washington Irving wrote the famous story about Rip Van Winkle, who slept for twenty years in the Catskill Mountains of New York State.

What West Coast state do dogs love to visit?

Collie-fornia. The tallest living things live in California, and you
can drive to visit them! (They're not dogs,
they're trees—the giant sequoias.)

How do kings and queens dine in North Dakota?

With Grand Forks. Just as two paths can come together and form a fork, rivers can make a fork too, as the Red Lake River and Red River do at the city of Grand Forks.

What's the Southwest state where a baker beats better batter?

New Mix-ico. You can bake in the sun in New Mexico, where summer temperatures are often over 90° Fahrenheit. Then you can cool off underground in the dramatic Carlsbad Caverns, where you can picnic a mile below the earth's surface.

What neighboring states are especially suitable for Christmas songs?

The Carol-inas. In North and South Carolina, carolers can sing in a wide range of settings, from picturesque mountains to spectacular seashore.

Why did the hot-dog roll go to Kentucky's capital?

To find a Frankforter. You can find yummy frankfurters in the city of Frankfort. Whatever you call them—frankfurters or franks, hot dogs, or wieners—Americans love them. In Kentucky you can munch on one while enjoying the famous Kentucky Derby horse race at Louisville.

How can a Salmon and a Snake get together in Idaho?

They're rivers! A real salmon doesn't often meet a real snake, but the rivers named after them join at Idaho's border with Oregon.

What do cats call a Hawaiian island?

Meowi! Maui is one of the biggest Hawaiian islands. The other large islands are Hawaii, Oahu, Kauai, Molokai, Lanai, Niihau, and Kahoolawe. There are also 124 small islands included in this state, which is located in the Pacific Ocean.

What is the East Coast's state of happiness?

Merry-land. Maryland is famous for its tasty crabcakes, which can make even crabby people joyful around dinnertime!

Who guards the Motor Speedway in Indiana?

Indiana-police officers. The city of Indianapolis (India-NAP-uh-liss), the state capital of Indiana, is where the famous 500-mile auto race is run every year.

What little purple fruit lives in New Hampshire's capital?

A Concord grape! Due to its varied climate, New Hampshire produces a wide variety of fruits, vegetables, trees, and other plants. The highest mountain in the Northeast is located here (Mount Washington, 6,288 feet high).

What Alabama city follows an auto?

Mobile! An automobile will give you the mobility to visit Alabama's Space and Rocket Center in Huntsville, cotton and peanut farms, cattle ranches, and fascinating Native American earth monuments at Moundville.

Which state has the tiniest soft drinks?

Mini-soda! Minnesota is where you can sip a soda near the source of the 'Sippi River. Minnesota's capital, St. Paul, is one of the "Twin Cities." Minneapolis lies across the Mississippi River from St. Paul.

How can you sail from Maine to Oregon and wind up in the same harbor?

Visit Portland. Two cities with the same name are Portland, Maine, on the Atlantic coast, and Portland, Oregon, on the Pacific coast. The shortest sailing distance between the Portlands (by way of the Panama Canal) is over 7,000 miles. However, if you fly over land, the two cities are about 2,500 miles apart.

Why do hens and chicks from Detroit love cars?

They're Mi-chickens! The state of Michigan is famous for its auto industry, centered in the city of Detroit, which started in 1899. You can visit the Henry Ford Museum in the Detroit suburb of Dearborn.

Where did the Texan get teed off?

Near the Golf of Mexico. If you play golf near the Gulf of Mexico, you may lose a lot of golf balls. They'll sink fast in this large body of water that borders Texas, Louisiana, Mississippi, Alabama, and Florida.

What states' names are good for a laugh?

Idaho-ho-ho, Oklaho-ho-homa, and Ha-ha-hawaii. Idaho is a big state (83,557 square miles) and so is Oklahoma (69,919 square miles). While they are both surrounded by land, Hawaii is a little state (6,471 square miles) surrounded by a lot of water (the Pacific Ocean).

Where does a pianist play in Florida?

At the Keys. The Florida Keys are a string of islands that are a favorite place for playing in the water. You can swim, water ski, snorkle, and scuba dive all year round.

Where do May flowers pop up in Illinois?

In Springfield! Springfield is the capital of Illinois, and the state flower is the violet, which does indeed show up every spring in great numbers. Many other states have cities or towns named Springfield too.

Why is the second-smallest state like a sandwich suit?

It's Deli-wear! You can buy a very tasty sandwich from a delicatessen in Delaware. Products from this state include chicken, ham, shellfish, fruits, and vegetables.

What Northwestern state has towns with ghostly sounds?

Moan-tana. In the 1800s prospectors looked for precious stones and gold in Montana. When they were gone, they left behind more than a hundred ghost towns, which you can visit—if you dare!

Why did the Newark soccer team look so sharp at practice?

They were in New Jerseys. The people of New Jersey can always use a lot of shirts. While it is one of the smallest states in size, New Jersey is one of the top ten in population.

What's for breakfast in a Georgia city?

Eggs and Macon! The city of Macon is right smack in the middle of Georgia, like the golden yolk in the middle of a fried egg! To the north of Macon is the site of America's first Gold Rush, at the town of Dahlonega.

What two Northern states are bundled up?

STATE LINE

The Da-coat-as. In North and South Dakota, you often need gloves, a hat, and a muffler as well as a coat to stay warm. Both states often have winter temperatures below 0° Fahrenheit!

What's the link between New York and Rhode Island?

The Connecticut connection. Connecticut joins the biggest and the smallest of the Northeastern states. The showman Phineas T. Barnum was born in Connecticut, and in the 1800s his famous three-ring circus included the "biggest elephant in the world," named Jumbo, and the "smallest man in the world," Tom Thumb.

Who designed a house for a Missouri mountain?

An Ozark-itect! The Ozark Mountains of southern Missouri seem designed for visitors who wish to hike up and down hills, canoe in fast streams, and swim in clear lakes.

What's for breakfast inside an Oregon volcano?

Crater Flakes. Crater Lake is a very big lake in the top of Crater Peak. A dormant (inactive) volcano, Crater Peak belongs to a group of volcanic mountains called the Cascade Range.

Why did Martha grow grapes on a Massachusetts island?

It was her Vineyard! Tourists and grapes can all bask in the sun
on tranquil Martha's Vineyard, off the coast of
Cape Cod, Massachusetts. You need to take a ferryboat to get to
Martha's Vineyard or the nearby island of Nantucket.

What Northern state do people dream of visiting?

Wish-consin. Wisconsin contains as many lakes as you could wish for. Besides bordering two of the Great Lakes, Lake Superior and Lake Michigan, it has thousands of smaller lakes.

Why do firefighters head for the hills of North Carolina?

They're the Great Smokies! You can often see a veil of mist hanging over the Great Smoky Mountains, part of the Appalachian Mountain range, which reaches from Alabama to Canada.

Where do ghosts hang out in California?

Death Valley. Death Valley is part of the Mojave (Mo-HA-vee) Desert and includes the lowest place in the United States (282 feet below sea level). Temperatures there can reach over 130° Fahrenheit and make you feel pretty low!

How scared is the forest in Arizona?

It's Petrified! Parts of ancient trees are found in the Petrified Forest National Park. Over millions of years, they have turned from wood into stone!

What's a 2,000-pound bather in the Potomac River?

A Washing-ton! In 1790, George Washington picked out the land where the capital city of the United States would be built. Washington, D.C. (District of Columbia), is located on the eastern bank of the Potomac River.

Where did the prospector look for gold in Wyoming?

In Yellowstone Park. Yellowstone National Park may not have any gold in it, but it is the location of the very famous geyser called Old Faithful.

What's the Eastern state that's just right for a writer?

State your name!

Pen!

Pencil-vania. Actually, Pennsylvania is named after a Penn! William Penn governed the region under British rule starting in 1681. Later, pens were used in Pennsylvania to sign the Declaration of Independence, and our Constitution was penned there too.

Why did a timid Little Rock from Arkansas go to Colorado?

To visit his Boulder cousin! Little Rock is the name of the capital of Arkansas (ARK-an-saw). The city of Boulder, and Colorado's capital city of Denver, are both very close to the Rocky Mountains.

What Central state needs a lot of lawn care?

Ne-grass-ka. Nebraska was one wide expanse of wild grasslands when wagon trains rolled through it in the 1800s. Now Nebraska's farmlands are important producers of corn and wheat.

What state do cars visit on vacation?

Road Island. It's an easy drive to the beach in Rhode Island, the smallest state of all. Strangely, it is not an island at all, despite its name. The next two smallest states are Delaware and Connecticut.

What Tennessee town makes you answer the door?

Knock-knocks-ville! When you knock on a solid wooden door, it just might be made from Tennessee lumber. Hardwood is shipped from four main river ports in Tennessee, including Knoxville.

What Central state is a big hit with baseball players?

Okla-homer. Oklahoma's most famous baseball player is Mickey Mantle, one of the top home-run hitters of all time. He played center field for the New York Yankees, and was voted Most Valuable Player three times (1956, 1957, 1962).

What Alaskan city has pretty snowdrifts?

Fairbanks. In the city of Fairbanks, banks of snow stay pretty frozen—the temperature sometimes reaches −70° Fahrenheit!

How did the Kansas Kid zigzag out of town so easily?

He was in Dodge City! In the 1800s, the state of Kansas was crowded with cowboys. There were so many in towns like Dodge City, Wichita, and Abilene that they became known as "cow towns"!

Why did the popcorn go for a swim in Utah's lake?

It had Great Salt! Utah's Great Salt Lake is all that's left of a great ocean that existed millions of years ago. Its salty water is so concentrated that it is more than four times saltier than any present-day ocean.

What famous explorer ended up in an Ohio town?

Columbus. Ohio's capital city carries his name, but Christopher Columbus never made it there. His voyages from Spain brought him to the islands of the West Indies. He never even set foot on the North American mainland.

Why did zany zebras zip and zoom down a Mississippi river?

It was the Ya-zoo! Lots of rainwater keeps the Yazoo River flowing in the state of Mississippi. Mississippi is one of the states with the highest annual rainfall.

What's the noise of a foghorn near Seattle, Washington?

A Puget Sound. You can sail a ship from Seattle, located on Puget (PYOO-jit) Sound, out to the waters of the Pacific Ocean. From there it's nearly 600 miles' sailing distance to Alaska, our most northern state.

What do you call a rhino from a Nevada town?

A Reno-cerous! During a hot, dry spell the residents of Reno can retire to nearby Lake Tahoe for a swim. (Nevada averages less rain than any other state—only four or five inches of rain in a whole year!)

What comes after warm Arkansas winters?

Hot Springs! The state of Arkansas is home to Hot Springs
National Park. People enjoy the forty-seven hot springs, with
natural water temperatures of 95° to 147° Fahrenheit.

What's New England's Christmas-tree state?

Fir-mont. In Vermont you can find evergreens, including several varieties of firs, as well as other trees such as the sugar maple, whose sap is made into tasty maple syrup.

What Eastern states sound like furry friends?

Fur-ginia and West Fur-ginia. All sorts of wild furry animals make their homes in the Appalachian Mountains of Virginia and neighboring West Virginia.

What are comic capers in New Orleans?

Louisi-antics! Folks in the state of Louisiana look forward to the annual Mardi Gras (MAR-dee Grah) parades. Dressed in outlandish costumes, people sing, dance, play music, and have a very jolly time!

What Iowa city sounds like tree frogs?

Cedar Ribbits! The city of Cedar Rapids is located on the Cedar River, which joins the Iowa River and flows into the Mississippi. Iowa's forests produce great quantities of red-cedar lumber.

When does a Great Lake think it's the greatest?

When it's feeling Superior. Lake Superior is the largest of the Great Lakes. It borders Canada, Minnesota, Michigan, and Wisconsin. Erie, Huron, Michigan, and Ontario are the other Great Lakes, and all five border on Canada.

What's the fastest mountain in South Dakota?

Mount Rushmore. People who visit South Dakota hurry to see this famous mountain. Carved into its side are the sculpted faces of four American presidents, *much* larger than life! The stone faces of George Washington, Thomas Jefferson, Abraham Lincoln, and Theodore Roosevelt are about six stories high!

What was the river called after the wedding?

Mrs. Sippi! The Mississippi River touches ten states and is
joined by many rivers, such as the Missouri River, as it winds its
way from Minnesota to the Gulf of Mexico.

Where do American snakes live?

In the USSSSSSSSA! Snakes live throughout North and South America, and most are very shy. If you ever see one, it will probably be sssssslipping away as fast as it can!

94-230

818
MAE

Maestro, Marco

Riddle City, USA

$14.89

DATE			
OC 12 94	SE 21 '95		
OC 20 94	NO 20 '95		
NO 3 94	NO 29 96	DE 04 97	
NO 17 94	DE 95	JA 9 98	
DE 2 '94	JA 4 '96		
JA 19 '95	FE 23 96	SE 23 98	
FE 23 '95	FE 29 96	DE 10 98	
MR 20 '95	MR 30 96	AP 9 '99	
AP 10 '95	MY 13 96		
AP 20 '95	SE 19 '96	OC 20 99	
MY 4 '95	OC 25 '96		
MY 25 '95	JA 31 '97